High Priestess of the Apocalypse: A Memoir of Disobedience

by

Christy Tending

ELJ Editions, Ltd. is committed to publishing works of quality and integrity. In that spirit, we are proud to offer this work of creative nonfiction to our readers; however, the story, the experiences, and the words are the individual authors' alone. The events are portrayed to the best of the individual authors' memory and some names and identifying details have been changed to protect the privacy of the people involved.

ISBN: 978–942004-70-7

Library of Congress Control Number: 2024936993

Cover Design by ELJ Editions, Ltd.

ELJ Editions, Ltd.
P.O. Box 815
Washingtonville, NY 10992
www.elj-editions.com

Praise for *High Priestess of the Apocalypse:
A Memoir of Disobedience*

"Christy Tending's exquisite book immerses you in a symphony of life's more poignant moments, painting scenes of everyday beauty and capturing the ephemeral hidden in the mundane. Alongside lies a deeper resonance—woven together are the threads of personal reflection and societal upheaval, inviting readers to confront the complexities of our world."

—Esmé Weijun Wang, author of *The Collected Schizophrenias.*

For Dan and Arlo, always and no matter what.

Table of Contents

"Nothing ever burns down by itself, every fire needs a little bit of help."
    —Chumbawamba

Introduction

Content Warning: This book contains themes of and references to violence and threats of violence, including police violence, colonialism, and interpersonal violence. This book also references drug and alcohol use, mental health issues, and suicidal ideation.

How do we meet the feeling that the world as we know it is ending? How do we maintain compassion for ourselves in the midst of grief and chaos? How do we inspire ourselves to action in the face of hopelessness designed to keep us complacent?

I have felt as though the world would end more times than I can count. This book draws on twenty-five years of Buddhism, twenty years of direct action experience, seven years of parenting, and a pervasive feeling that I still have no idea what I'm doing. It is about the looming humanitarian crisis we face in the form of the rapidly changing climate, except where it is also about place, memory, parenting, sobriety, cats, hummingbirds, Buddhism, death, and disability. It is about the humanity of those who are fighting for a new world. It is about my child and the next generation, as well as a broken inheritance that we have collectively picked up in a bum deal. It is about resilience and hope in the face of that. The title is both a little tongue and cheek, as well as a serious endeavor: how do we, as spiritual beings, preside over what feels like a daily ending-of-the-world.

I cannot and do not pretend to speak for the climate movement: we are a diverse and amorphous and decentralized movement. Our experiences are not all the same. I can speak only for my own experience, even as I recognize myself as a cell in the ecosystem of this movement that I call my political home. My intention is not to speak for the climate movement, but to refract some light through the experience of my political life.

There are enormous gaps in my memory. Places where grief and trauma have wiped the years away, like scraping away the hearts drawn in condensation. None of this is exact. Names have been changed and people have been anonymized to protect their identities and privacy. Their beating hearts are in this book, however, I assure you. The book is in roughly chronological order except where it isn't.

Except for the places where the book borrows memory from itself or loops back to point to something again. Look again, it wants to say. Who am I to deny it? Events have been compressed, consolidated, or expanded; some have been skipped over and others are explored more than once. Details have been embellished. I have speculated, imagined, and outright invented sections (because that is what life feels like when you live in your head sometimes). But even in those places, this is what feels true to me.

This book is ultimately about ways that we can move forward empowered by community and the inspiration that strikes in moments of interconnection. It is about how we choose to gather our own strength in the face of fear and what often feels like the end of the world.

The antidote might be wonder. The secret answer might be refusing to buckle to inevitability, even as we embrace nonattachment. This book is, in many ways, unfinished. Because that is the nature of life and our collective work toward justice.

This is a love story. If you are reading this, we are now a part of each other's story. Thank you.

Memoir is Erasure Poetry

Fetch me the Exact-O knife.

There is no way to capture the whole experience. Thousands of photographs later, and I am still writing myself toward my life. I am sitting in front of a blank page, trying to explain what it feels like. The texture of it, the temperature, the wash of color. Although it feels more like a wall of text, and I am cutting most of it away until what it left feels true and kind and real.

Memoir cannot account for every eventuality without heaving under the burden of endless caveat—nor does it serve solely as an indictment. Just because I tell you that the white pony loved to roll around in the creek doesn't mean that I've forgotten my grandmother's applesauce cake. I remember Old Bay seasoning dripping down my arms on the screened-in porch, and I remember my hands shaking as I read my vows. I am cutting away what doesn't matter to point you toward a narrative that will make sense. I am scooping all of it together under the blanket fort. I am making room for the monsters under the bed.

I can tell you things from my perspective, but that perspective is unreliable, at best, and certainly incomplete. I have forgotten certain things on purpose, like the broken wine glass and the empty, heavy silence of grudges. The heat on my face when, wordless, I know what I've done. I want to know how much of this is mine to tell: how much of it happened to me and how much of it was a matter of proximity? How much of my story is mine to tell and how much should I excise, whether single words or entire paragraphs, letting bits of it flutter to the floor?

I can tell you how I felt, and I'd dare you to try to stop me. That part is mine.

But what about the name I gave my child? Round and soft, with a bit of a thrum. The middle name is more angular, the letters that leap, and the way the sound of it pulls your lips into a smile. The two names together make a little song that we sing all day long in our house, gliding up and down the stairs. The name means dinner is ready and I love you and one more hug. I gave the name away; it isn't mine to own or to tell. It's his to do with what he wants now.

I am trying to write about my life, and keep stumbling into other peoples' stories, the ones that don't belong to me, the ones I only heard from the next room, the ones I promised to protect. Sometimes, it's to keep them safe from themselves and their worst choices. Sometimes from the world that wouldn't understand—because once it's out there, you cannot control how you're interpreted.

That's different from keeping someone's story out of fear of their anger: the ones who use the truth as a weapon and wield emotion as obfuscation. The ones who erase not to illuminate something bigger, but to stamp you out completely. The ones who claim your story for themselves, casting themselves as the main character and using sleight of hand to make it fit.

This is about the way secrets oxidize when they hit the page: the way they turn to poison in the light or the way they turn black and scab over, finally ready to heal from the inside. The others? They don't get to choose.

What am I trying to say? That I don't want to forget listening to Prince in the hospital when he was born.

That I am a free woman—which is to say: *not in prison*—because people kept their mouths shut. They didn't feel the need to go blabbing every detail.

This is a memoir, not a map of where the bodies are buried, but the memory of the music I heard as the wind blew through the trees in the graveyard. It is about Delaware in January and leaving my grandmother's ashes in their final place, as though anything to do with the sea is final. It's about wringing out everything into the sink and watching what floats to the surface.

It is a hermit crab, like the ones in the tourist shops, or it is a recipe for applesauce cake, or an erasure poem, taking out the bits that don't make sense (which is most of it) and rearranging it into something that someone can understand or relate to, blurring out the faces and focusing in on the tiniest details. The sound of his laugh, like a bird that's yet to be named. His feet crashing down the stairs, like ripe plums falling to earth. The stack of books we have read and re-read, the smell of the paper and his hair against my cheek. I close my eyes and memorize it. Soft, crisp.

I have practiced shame so many times that I often wonder if there's anything at all worth saying. This is how we become erased. In those tiny moments of "Who the fuck do you think you are?" as you are falling asleep and remembering the terrible thing I probably did at the sleepover in fourth grade when I was trying to grow up and be loved. In trying to be careful, I sometimes lose another word that might have mattered. The whiteout splatters, collateral damage, onto something I wanted to keep.

I will redact the mundane details, but there are salacious bits I want to tell you. All the salacious and dangerous things like jumping off cliffs and the way I drove a van into a ditch once. The things I've lit on fire, not the least of which was my own life, when I decided that I could not be with someone who couldn't summon passion for me. The way he demanded that I stifle my own passions, the fact that I felt ravenous toward the world shamed him.

I will not tell you his name, but I can tell you about the way the light hit my pink hair one afternoon in the park and I knew myself as a microscopic god, a tiny spec of omniscient moss in an infinite universe.

I am telling you that I am still willing to be broken open.

I want to show you the precarious, liminal moments: all the animals I have held as their bodies died, and how I whispered how good they were, how loved, how safe. How the last thing they heard was the story of how well they were loved told back to them. There is something comforting about hearing your own story told back to you, just the sweet parts. "Just the good bits, you remember? Only the parts where you were loved."

We are told not to speak ill of the dead. My father's father is not a part of my story. He erased himself from my father's life and I will not hold him in esteem simply because he is in the ground. This is memoir as erasure poetry, too: withholding a story to strip it of its power. Once they're in the ground, have they left those stories for us to tell? Or do the stories die, too, entombed like golden scarabs or food on which the dead will feast for eternity? Do our stories finally unravel from one another? Is death the moment we can finally drag it all into the light?

Life is pockmarked with these kinds of loss, made more devastating by the fact that it was never the salacious bits that mattered. It was the ordinary days that made up a life, listening to the cat snoring in her crate and buying milk and listening to the coffee being made. Today, the sun filtered through the olive tree in the backyard and we ate dinner on the porch. My child's face was stained with strawberries and he snuggled into my arms when the wind picked up.

This memoir is an erasure poem, or a hunt for pirate treasure.

Alive

Put me on the edge of annihilation, and I will love you forever. I will supplicate myself before you, dear world, for a taste of it. It does not matter what kind of death: of the body or of the ego. One is not more painful than the other: I am a connoisseur of the ill-advised. I may as well have been raised by wolves and broken glass. This is how I move through the world, cloaked only in illusion and muscle memory.

The time I was not eaten by a trash-grubbing bear in the middle of the night, banging my silly pot in the middle of the woods, mostly naked. Because he had filled up on garbage, there was no room for me. The winter days I do not crash into the woods: carving my skis against the hill, edging the snow and narrowly dodging head trauma. I sail on my own breath and a belief in my body.

One summer, my sister's horse galloped alongside mine, and we flew across Wyoming. Arms out, hips rooted; if the horse hit a gopher hole, I was done-for.

When the cops in tactical gear do not beat me into the pavement, but my cheeks are a swamp from tear gas and adrenaline. Leaping off a cliff—again, mostly naked—into a Canadian lake where no one would have found my body. I missed its jagged bits by a few inches, which is to say: enough.

The times my child holds my hand without warning and his sweaty paw slips into mine, he smiles up at me with a face like the sky. I am eviscerated: reduced to smoldering ash where I stand. In the brilliance of his luminescence, I cease to exist. I try to forget that the act of ushering him into life nearly ended us both: this is what it is to be alive. Allow me to meet all the bears face to face in the darkness. Permit me one more cliff before I go.

A Name Like a Flying Cheesecake

I like the providence of names. Move a letter here or there, or leave them as they were, and they come to mean a whole new person. The name itself takes on a new life: wearing its old coat with a new brooch or a fresh lining. It sits in restaurants the old name never knew, watches sunsets like they're the first. My name came from Christa. Or Krista. I'm not sure which. But Christa or Krista was a German friend of my mom's, whom mom met when she was living in a VW camper somewhere along a highway between somewhere in Switzerland and somewhere in Germany. Who can say? It was the 70's. I only have one story about Krista or Christa, and I turn it over in the palm of my hand like a coin I found in the pocket of the old coat of my name. For decades now, I have worn it until the cuffs are threadbare. I have turned it over in my palm until the coin is smooth with use.

But the story is like this. One day, Krista's friend baked her a cheesecake—her favorite—but she had no other way to get it home, so she secretly packed the cheesecake into the shelf underneath the back windshield of her husband's precious BMW, the one in which no food was allowed, the one that meant more to him than his own life, and when he hit the brakes, you know what happened next. The cheesecake launched itself from its cardboard box face first into the inside of the front windshield of the beloved BMW.

I don't know how that story ends, whether he yelled or laughed, but either way, Krista died in childbirth some time later. I think about the stories her overly serious husband told their daughter about her mother. I wonder whether the little girl, who is all grown up now, knows about the cheesecake. I wonder about the fun she might have had at the expense of her father's BMW. I don't know how that story ends, either.

But I think about my name, not so many letters removed, and sometimes I imagine my name as the flying cheesecake, caught midair on the Autobahn, in the slice of a moment before it becomes a punchline. I imagine looking at the dessert against the glass in gaping-mouthed shock, and doing the only sensible thing one can—before I dissolve into laughter.

I swipe my finger through the creamy cheesecake filling, with the warmth of Madagascar vanilla and a breath of lemon zest, and lift it to my tongue. I taste the sweetness of my namesake and the tang of my birthright.

Roots, Seven Through Fourteen

*S*even

In the summer, I learned to ride horses. My favorite was a large bay named Luna, who was gentle and patient. In the winter, I learned to ski. I fell in love with both as they were far more dangerous than anything else my school or peers could offer me. These moved me farther and farther from kids my own age, but closer to the world. The snow, the deer, and the backwoods they call home. My childhood smells like horses and hay. It sounds like the rushing wind and snow falling on pine trees. It is the music of yellow leaves, touching briefly as they flutter to the ground in autumn. It was a slow process of falling in love and driving home in the dark.

At forty, when I walk into a barn, I swoon at the smell.

Ten

My school had rules for birthday parties: you could invite the whole class, just the boys, or just the girls. A boy in my fifth grade class decided to invite only the boys to his birthday party. The unspoken thing: he didn't break any rules, he was just being shitty. Like so much of the patriarchy. Not against the rules, but shitty. I draw a line in the sand. When it was time for my birthday party, I invited only the girls to my pool party. Fuck that kid and his father's Honda dealership. I said, It's only fair.

And, unaccustomed to fairness as an argument, another kid told me I was inviting only the girls because I want to see them in their bathing suits. *Because you're a dyke*, he said. His older brother taught him that word. On the car ride home, I asked my mother what dyke means. She told me it's a nasty word for women who love other women.

This means there is a love that's wrong, somehow, and this boy found it. Why is it insulting if it's true?

Eleven

In the photograph of Rachel Carson I chose for my school project, she is wearing a jean jacket and glancing over her shoulder, unsmiling, binoculars over her shoulder. You could have mistaken her for joyless. But she loved the sea, do you understand? It obsessed her with its power and delicate details. She worshiped the little tide pools, with ink-black urchins; and she longed to understand the tides themselves—and the earth—so much that she rooted out death with her bare hands. She could not abide the quiet longing of the flowers, sitting attentively on their branches, unpollinated in a season that demands it. Do you understand? She could not withstand a lack of bees. She couldn't leave well enough alone, and it killed her. I learned that this is what it is, sometimes, to love the world.

To hold it so fiercely that it devours you. To threaten power so completely that they come for your reputation when they cannot destroy your will.

Twelve

My shaking hands and I were talking about gorillas and forests, but I did not know what I was unleashing in myself, I promise. In front of the whole school, I talked about Dian Fossey, like I knew what I was doing. Like I knew how far I was willing to go, what I was prepared to risk. When I talk about what it is to love, I am talking about intimacy. When you get close enough to something, you either find yourself either bored to tears, or prepared to burn everything else to the ground for it. When I am practicing for my talk, I visit the gorillas at the zoo often enough that one day, as I walk into the house and sit down next to the glass, the silverback sits down next to me, munching leaves, snuggling as close as he can but for the indestructible barrier.

Here is what I know, but do not say: Dian Fossey died for love.

Fourteen

In 1997, I watched the egret stretch its feet though the water where Coyote Creek meets Richardson Bay, all sleek yellow legs and a decisive countenance, stalking something, and I decided I wanted to move to California. In Marin County, everything smells like salt and redwood trees. The fog swoops in each morning and every afternoon to coddle my broken brain. I decided I never want to leave. This was only my first trip to California with my mother and sister on spring break, and I was hooked. We ate blueberry pancakes at a little cafe every morning and spent our days driving winding roads that offer the untold. I have always been a nerd for nature; environmentalism was not cool in 1997. This place may as well have nailed my foot to the earth. I sobbed on the plane ride home.

That summer, I was diagnosed with clinical depression.

I moved to California four years and five months later.

Coyote Smile

Mine is the father who has gifted me far more pocket knives in this lifetime than dolls.

The one who brags to anyone who will listen that I'm a prettier skier than he is. He tells them that, faced with a cliff, I'm effortless. Perhaps the only time he's called me pretty, because in his mind, what difference would my prettiness have made in the world? Or in his? None at all, of course. He preferred the tough daughter. So I became, to my own amazement and delight, the "rub some dirt on it" daughter, the "take no shit" daughter, the "never surrender" daughter.

This is who I imagine myself to be. If he is Zeus, I am his Artemis, made holy by my wildness: the coyote who grins as it trots along the side of the road.

The Ones for Luck

I remember everything smelling like sawdust and honeysuckle and white paint. I remember everything swelling like a thunderstorm, the underside of each blade of grass bright like lightning.

When I left Maryland, knowing I was surrendering it as home, I took the corner of the paddock with me. The barren one. The one worn from hoofbeats. The one whose gate I could still unlock in my sleep. (Unclip the nickel bolt snap and unwrap the chain from the gate, but not the fence post. Shimmy your right shoulder underneath the rung on the aluminum gate—second or third from the top—and lift the gate away from the divot in the earth. Now you can swing it open just enough to slide through.)

And I know this even though the paddock and the gate and the chain and the lock were all demolished twenty years ago to make space for a McMansion development that seized its place in the world in the name of capital and interior decorating. But when I'm at the dentist or on meditation retreat or trying to come back to the safety of a happy place within the memory of my body, I conjure that patch of land, paddock splayed out on the hill and valley below, underneath blue summer sky with the smell of freshly nibbled grass and the slick of horse sweat and the saturation of dust in the air clinging to humidity right before a thunderstorm. I remember and return.

In my memory, I am holding a cotton leadshank which I used to need before I taught my horse to heel. His face rests against my right shoulder, and I cluck softly to tell him to match my stride when he gets distracted by chickens. I soften when I remember my harsh tone the time I told him to back up and stand all 900 pounds behind me when we saw a coyote on the trail; I dismounted and had a branch in my hand before I knew what I was doing. I remember his gray face, his deep eyes which would light up at the sound of my voice and the way he would come running up the hill and stop inches from my hands, outstretched to gather him close, wind lifting around him like magic, present and hopeful and happy to see me. His chest was soft and smooth and where he liked best to be petted. His forelock swiped over one eye, hiding the forehead he used to rub against my ribcage, satisfying an itch or maybe just saying Hello, I love you.

I remember driving to the barn on high school winter mornings to break up ice in the buckets so the horses would have something to drink and how their blankets would trap their warmth against their enormous bodies. And I remember climbing aboard my horse in the snow, his horseshoes anointed with tungsten carbide to grip the slick trail. I remember our flight through the woods at dawn in January. I felt like I was perched on the moon, the silver light of my beloved friend glinting between naked black trees, me digging my heels in, and lifting both our faces as we sailed over fences.

Now, I'm thinking about the kind of equipment they would have used to pull up hundreds of fence posts to make the land more open and I wonder if the ground had time to heal at all before they sliced into it to dig foundations for rec rooms crouched under formal dining rooms stretched beneath en-suite bathrooms. The irony of the development, of course, is that they put all those houses in the way of such a beautiful view.

I remember that the view held emptiness not like sadness, but like a bell. I remember the way the sky would gather weather in its fists. And the way we could beat the rain to the barn if we lifted our faces toward the west at just the right moment and knew what corn smells like in an approaching storm.

What I don't remember is how I held the rage at those who had no connection to the land—who did not raise themselves from the threshold before adolescence into adulthood on the trails or leaping over coops between fields. I don't know which drawer stores my anger, but it feels swelled shut, and I try not to drive past the farm anymore. I don't remember how I cupped the helplessness in my hands without it slipping between my fingers. I don't remember how I reconciled being so busy blocking logging roads in Canada or campaigning to protest Indigenous rights in Indonesia that I failed to protect this one tract. I don't remember how I've ever justified picking my battles.

I don't remember the last day or where all the horseshoes went: the bent and mangled ones, the ones for luck.

Delaware Winter

for Betty

We are leaving my grandmother's ashes, shaking them from their tin evenly under the boardwalk, where we used to put her beach chair, once her shrunken, varicose legs could no longer carry her across the sand.

She would toss pieces of molding bread for sea-gulls. Delighted by their screeching, she laughed loudly, with her smoker's rasp. Once spread, shook out under rotting planks, my father makes no move to comfort me. I slip the toe tag into a back pocket. Eventually the wind picks up and we wince against it. We stand, planted over her—now among Delaware frost.

We lock eyes and laugh dryly in commiseration, wondering how long before we may return to the car.

Pink Hair

The first time I had pink hair, I brought a sprig of bougainvillea I had snipped, guerilla-style, from the wall between the Safeway and the Muni tracks at Church and Market Streets in the Castro. The same Safeway where I had purchased the ingredients to make grilled cheese after closing down the bar and Pied Piper-ed my friends back to my apartment to make food at 3am because I did not want to feel lonely. The same Safeway where I ended up too many times after too many drinks making too much trouble. There was the incident with the almond butter, of course.

I had fallen in love with the rich magenta of bougainvillea in Peru, where they climbed over whitewashed walls in Miraflores, the color haunting my dreams, the spiky thorns along the vine snagging my attention and sometimes a thumb when I tried to pick the flowers. So when I wanted to dye my hair, there was only one color I could think of to emulate: the bougainvillea. Beautiful and dangerous.

At the time, I was working on a campaign to pressure Victoria's Secret to use recycled content in their catalogs, which might seem like small potatoes, but they send out a million catalogs a day, so maybe not? They were sourcing their paper from Northern Canada, endangered woodland caribou habitat and the traditional lands of First Nations communities that had no say in whether their sacred land and their sacred trees were being pulped into junk mail. On that campaign, I led dozens of disruptive actions at Victoria's Secret locations all over the Bay Area. My pink hair became a feature, matching the brand's color perfectly. And becoming a beacon. We'll meet up at the corner of X and Y streets. Look for the person with bright pink hair. I was my own personal rallying cry.

One day, waiting for the bus, a little girl shyly approached me at her father's urging and asked if she could ask me a question, secretly. (Obviously, yes.) "Are you a mermaid," she asked. "Yes," I replied. She wanted it to be true, and I didn't see any harm in letting it be. Wasn't I some mystical creature? Imagining a new world where the trees stand in their homes and the river remains unchallenged and the caribou migrate along the same route where they have migrated since time immemorial? If I were a mermaid, perhaps I would have some power. As the little girl ran giggling back to her dad, he mouthed the words, "Thank you." I will never know what my little white lie meant to either of them. At the time, it just felt like an easy kindness.

Another day, I spent an afternoon high on shrooms in Golden Gate Park, seeing my glittering hair with the light streaming through it, feeling the smell of the redwood trees inside my skin. When it began to rain, my hair was lightening.

It was with pink hair that I learned to become a comfortable public speaker; that I learned how to launch a balloon banner without getting pinched by mall security; that I learned that being pinched by mall security wasn't a big deal. Perhaps it would have happened anyway. Or perhaps the pink hair was the crucible I needed to become the next iteration of myself, the mark of someone who was prepared to stand out and rise against. My pink hair was a rebel's armor, but when I grew it out, the armor remained.

At nearly forty, I returned to the color. Because life is too short. Because I long to be a mermaid again. The color does not match a corporate target, but instead the color of the future I want: bright, unmistakable; unapologetically, deeply, femme and anarchist. The electric pink hides the small amount of danger I still keep in my back pocket. The children at school pickup ask if I am a mermaid. I tell them yes. That they can be mermaids, too. That they can imagine a new world.

Ten Things That Will Happen in College

1. You will get arrested for the first time, under the disdainful eye of the Victoria's Secret regional manager. Upon seeing you chained to the front of the store chanting about trees, she will sigh, roll her eyes, and say, "Oh, it's you," crossing her arms over her smart black blazer.

2. But first, you will teach others on your dorm floor how to do laundry. How to separate the loads—what needs cold water and what wants hot. How to measure and where to pour the soap. How to remove clothes from the dryer right away, warm. How to hold them to your face and breathe, though that isn't part of doing laundry. But isn't it?

3. You will navigate public transit home from the Castro on Halloween while rolling on MDMA with your friend, all wigs and shouting. You will learn to find your way using the hills and the stars as guides, even though they double themselves as you hold yourself against a lamppost. You will know that sometimes shame smells like coconut rum.

4. You will let Eva Hesse save your soul more than once. You will come to understand that bell hooks and Angela Davis have the answer for everything. You will let Fiona Apple and Tracy Chapman rock you to sleep. You will have your fake ID confiscated at the Yeah Yeah Yeahs show at Great American Music Hall, but you will not hold that against them. You will discover that you are more of a Brontë sisters person than a Jane Austen person, which is saying a lot.

5. You will smoke clove cigarettes under the neon signs in the Mission, the smoke curling into a vision of your future like a horoscope, while you wait for the bus on an inappropriate street corner, electricity crackling overhead.

6. You will stare down the man in workshop who describes the poem about your grandmother's death as being "not credible." Your face will grow hot, its own incredulity. In that moment, you will grow up and resolve to be more choosy about the people you fuck. You will struggle to imagine the future: that you will find a life that is everything you could possibly want.

7. You will feel tempted to become a religion major, a pull that will make no sense to you as an agnostic. The only gods you have known have been horses and the sound of their hooves splashing through creeks.

8. You will feel kinship with your elderly Irish Catholic World Religion professor, and will be drawn in by his warmth, a grandfather free from disdain, the grandfather you did not have.

9. It will make no logical sense to you, until you discover that you are the Buddhist you will write term papers about. You will practice the bliss of sitting in silence, watching the breath that breathes you. You will embrace the agony of aching knees as you watch your spinning, obsessive thoughts and try not to hate them. You will learn that your love of trees and the moon is not merely an exercise as a poet, not only something to digest and regurgitate for a writing workshop.

10. You will discover that everything is holy. This will happen, too.

It Explodes

Did you know that when you pour water onto a can full of boiling oil, it explodes? The oil explodes, I mean. The water evaporates. I don't remember what happens to the can.

We spend all day breaking the law. At night, we build fires, watch things burn, so tired of being serious little outlaws.

Listen.

If you're going to be defiant, you need to keep it buttoned up. Be cool when the cops drive by. Stay quiet around people you don't know. Turn your phone off unless you want the feds to hear you. Slip behind a tree when the helicopters hover overhead. Keep your head down when they're taking pictures, trying to figure out what you're up to. Don't talk about the time and place.

Tell the people in town you're a student, visiting family, on a camping trip. Be friendly, but don't make friends. Order pancakes without bacon, but don't tell them you're a vegetarian. Change the subject. Check your taillights. Watch for moose. They'll tell you moose work alone, but I've seen a pair of them that would demolish your car if you're not looking both ways. Drive with the windows down. Remove the SIM card.

Bathe in the lake before dawn. This was my favorite part: cool breathing, mist sulking on the surface, my heartbeat in my ears, looking up at the golden sky. Don't forget this part. Don't rush it. Listen to the loons sing as you dress on the shore. Burn leeches off your legs with a lighter, before you wend your way through the forest, up the muddy hill, ready for work. Chop wood wearing flip-flops. (You probably shouldn't, but it's been known to happen.)

Make a cup of Nescafe in a tin cup and take it on the road with you. Hang one arm out the window, drape one wrist over the steering wheel. Steer with your knees. Pull over for a dip in the lake with long-needled pine trees. The one like glass, the one where I know someone who drank Guinness for breakfast. Like a person could forget something like that.

Run away, knowing that you'll end up right back here. Walk down the old logging road before the light leaves. Take long drags, leaning against the bulldozer they forgot to claim. Ash into the sandpit. Burn cigarette marks into the soles of your disintegrating shoes.

Don't be afraid of the bears. They'll wander into the camp kitchen, but they're only looking for leftovers. Bang on pots and pans, naked, when they wake you in the middle of the night. They'll wander back into the forest.

Wear a skirt or the same pair of jeans that's losing structural integrity in the knees. The ones with soot stains down the front. Just nothing flashy, keep it simple. Nothing to draw attention to yourself. Don't spread out. Don't take up space until it's time to take up a whole highway full space. Know when it's time.

Write the number on your arm or your leg so you know who to call from the payphone. Try not to get arrested with the bail money. I'm trying to remember everything.

The blackflies drone as we stand watch. Ancient truck tracks have vanished after years of insistence. No one gets through. Leap off the cliff, because this might be your only chance. Because you might want to tell your children about this someday. Because this is what it is to live a life of risk.

When you break the law all day, you really need to let your hair down at night. Sing loudly in the dark forest, even if you only have a single guitar between you. Tell ghost stories about your friends. Make things explode like a can of oil shattering into fractals. Let the night confiscate your shame.

How to Freehand a Banner

If you can get Lynn or David to do it, that's your best bet. If you have a projector, that's a distant second-best. If you do not have to freehand your banner, all the better.

If you are going the not-Lynn-or-David, decidedly second-best route:

Hang your banner fabric on the largest wall you can find. Depending on how large you want your banner, you might have to do it in sections. Project the digital image of what you want your banner to look like onto the fabric. Trace it from the projection. Then lay the banner flat and paint it. It sounds simple, but it's time consuming. I've wrecked a good percentage of my knees crouching on concrete to paint banners over the years. Please leave time for it to dry. This will depend on the time of year and the humidity of your climate. But as long as you don't fold it when wet, it will be close to exact.

But if that is not an option and you must freehand your banner:

Maybe you do not have electricity, let alone a projector, you will have to freehand your banner. Maybe you don't have a tall enough wall or a laptop to draw up the image. You will have to go the rough and tumble route, and embrace it as a very imprecise science. It will have a very human touch. Perhaps, looking at the photograph decades later, you will appreciate that. You will remember that it was you who painted those tall letters and you will forgive yourself for those jagged edges. Your arms will ache at the curve of the S, compacted by the ache of your knees and the compression of time that tells you that, at midnight, with the action the next day, it just has to fucking get done, okay?

Decide on your slogan. If it is a very tall banner, you might divide it into multiple lines with big bold words. If it is a very long banner to go widthwise across a logging road, you might be able to manage a long phrase. Something connected to your demand set. Here is what we want, your banner will say. There will not be room to explain why the things we want are sacred. What they mean to our hearts. The sound of wonder our child made when he first spotted the hummingbird. The look of fear when he saw the clouds of smoke and the orange sky. The banner does not have the space to explain all of this.

We hope that simple words will be enough. We hope that inconvenience will have its intended effect.

Divide the banner into sections for each row, then each word, then each letter. The math is not perfect. I's are more narrow than an S, of course. Leave the spaces between the words a bit bigger than you think. Let the words breathe the way the land is gasping for air. The way the people are fighting to breathe and afford food. Make each letter a bit fatter than you think it should be. They need substance to be legible. They need the richness and luxury of sticking their elbows out a bit, unbuttoning the top button as they curl up on the couch for a nap.

Hope and pray the banner will be dry enough in time to load into the car. Cross your fingers for wind. Hold your talismans and invite evaporation.

§

Last night, I helped my child make his first picket sign to support his chosen uncle, who is on his third day of a strike. I explained that there would be picket signs waiting for us, but my son wanted to make his own. He wanted to use his own words. He wanted to carry a thing that he made.

He gave me the message and I showed him how to divide the side of an old box into three neat rows, sketching them with pencil onto cardboard. I show up how to divide up the words, to count up the letters, sketching those onto each of their rows. From there, my child colored in the letters, making them deep blue for UC Berkeley. He added a train, as well, at the bottom. These striking workers are not part of the railroad, my son just likes trains. He thought trains would be nice.

He wanted his sign to make people smile. Joy is what we fight for, too.

If I had given us time like a river

There is the part that definitely happened. There are all the parts that had to happen. There are certainties scorched into my memory that couldn't have happened any other way. There are the parts that set off a cascade of conditional reasoning.

If our eyes had met in the Greyhound parking lot at midnight; if we'd used the car as a speaker and swam in the lake; if we scraped scales off the fish; if I had watched you chop wood; if I had let those same hands hold me; if we'd eaten blueberries right off the bush; if we'd jumped off the cliff more than once; if I'd learned how to properly remove muskrat pelts, slicing through sinew; if you'd sat across from me eating eggs in the vinyl booth; if I took it as a victory when I made you smile; if I laughed when you laughed; if I fried the fish over a campfire in my flip-flops; if we'd followed the moose into the trees with our eyes; if you'd hidden me in the forest until I turned to moss; if we'd snuck cigarettes from a plastic bag; if my clothes turned to dust; if I hung my hand out the driver's side window, ashing into the wind; if I'd learned the new words to old songs; if I'd drive with my knees with Nescafe in the cupholder; if I'd trusted you to make the coffee and drive the car sometimes so I could lean against the cool window in silence.

That is the story of how we became friends. It is not a metaphor, but action. This is what we did—or part of it. A fragment of a hidden history. I was deported and the rest of it was cut short. I went back to America and you went up the river.

But show me what else could it have been: the unwritten part, the unspoken speculation. I don't know. Perhaps there are too many unknowns. Too many uncertainties.

If gotten into the boat with you; if we'd zipped under the bridge as the sirens crested the hills; if I'd put the tent stakes back into the soft earth; if I had looked up at the Northern Lights knowing they were welcoming me home; if I defied the court order; if I had violated deportation; if there had been no court order; if there had been no deportation; if you'd kissed me like the cops were coming; if we'd watched the sky in silence; if we'd watched the eagles slice across it; if I'd watched as the rest of the group drove away into the night; if you'd put your arm around me and said Come here; if we'd watched until the sky went completely dark; if we'd set out the next morning into the bright water, the electric sky; if I had leaned against you in the back of the boat, listening to the Evinrude transport us into a different dimension; if we'd taken apart the abandoned machinery; if we'd made something new from it instead; if I'd give us time like a river; if I had learned to gut and skin the deer myself; if I had learned how to take the entire animal to pieces; if I had stayed for the winter and used the snowshoes we made; if you'd used your name for me that only you used; if I'd been brave enough to stay or brave enough to stay, depending on whether you're talking about the bridge or the land itself, then what?

That is the part I cannot know. This is the part no one can tell me, even years later. I can only imagine what would have happened next. I can only fill in the gaps from my projections. I can only write out a new beginning that we'll never have.

In my mind, I flow up an infinite river of possibility. Of choose-your-own-adventure. Of turn to page whatever.

The Trouble With Little Violence

I would never actually hit you, he told me. As if it were obvious. As if that was the line. I sat on the counter staring at him. I had recoiled when he punched the cabinet, feeling the wind of his fist in my ear. I'm not sure, in retrospect, if I was challenging him or simply too shocked to speak or look anywhere else. I looked into his face, searching for a shred of what wasn't there. He looked into my face in return, registering my fear, becoming angrier. Furious I had responded to this outburst. His embarrassment only fed his rage. I would never actually hit you.

In my life there has been big violence and little violence. The big violence is, strangely, easier to talk about: the big, showy, state-sponsored violence is easy to see. Look, there is the tear gas, here are the flash-bangs.

I can demonstrate it: my right shoulder still doesn't move properly after a cop dislocated it. I can remember the dirt road in Canada where it happened, I can explain what it's like to be surveilled by helicopters for days on end at a logging blockade. Somehow, the violence and the invasive violation of having my phone tapped sparks a bigger reaction. The big violence—of having loved ones arrested and jailed, of the weight of a found rubber bullet in my hand, of telling my body not to run when that's all it wants to do—this is easier to explain. The way I've been handcuffed and left in the back of a van with no air conditioning, please understand.

The little violence looked like this: I would never actually hit you. (Although, his fist had just connected with the cupboard a few inches from my face, so forgive my confusion.) And the violence looked like his dead expression when he learned he was the one who made me recoil in fear. The little violence sounds like, What's the big deal?

The way I became smaller and smaller, until I could fit in the palm of your hand. Until I was sweet, pocket-sized.

If it was real, I was supposed to have a black eye, to have something to show for it. To be real, it needed to be big. I was supposed to have earned this pain. That would make it glorious and believable. Instead, the violence was so small from the outside, it was almost microscopic. You needed to get close to see it, which is why by the end, I barely had any friends besides the truly persistent. If he let me have friends, it stood to reason, they would get close enough to see the truth. His friends were my friends, he argued. And I didn't argue back.

One day, lying on his bed, I was reading *Ecology Against Capitalism*—I will never forget this; my dog-eared copy is still on my bookcase after 16 years. He asked me what I was reading and I showed him the book. He asked what it was about and I read him a recently highlighted bit. For school or for fun? It was a little bit of both.

You shouldn't do that, he said. It makes me feel stupid, like I'm not as smart as you. As he'd promised, he did not hit me, but stalked out of the room, enraged. I heard him banging around in the kitchen a few seconds later. This is little violence, of course: a tiny, but cruel act of trying to make me smaller and less bright. It took years to convince me this would have been enough to leave him right then. This is the trouble with little violence: it takes so much more convincing it is wrong.

His words picked at my skin until I was invisibly bloodied. Sometimes, I could laugh them off. See? I could say with my fake face, I am unbothered. I can love your cruelty, which means, perhaps, I am also loveable? The question mark, hanging in the air, hoping he would swoop it out of the way and say he was kidding. (Which, it should seem plainly obvious, never happened.)

This was little violence: no flash-bangs or pepper spray or nights in jail. This little violence looked like fury when I didn't answer my phone. It felt like being accused of sleeping with my friends until I could count them on one hand. It was the slow wearing-down of a person who is ignored and treated as disposable, until she is needed for something specific, in which case she is expected to be present and cheerful.

It's not like I ever hit you, he says when I tell him I'm unhappy.

It is little violence, as though that's true—as though that matters. It is little violence, still trying to convince myself all these years later. But it is not. It is no small thing, this erosion of self. It is little-ing: making me smaller and smaller. It is not little, but belittling.

And what about my own violence? The way I abandoned myself on the side of the road in the middle of the night. The way I let my small, young self believe she deserved it. I gave up on the unwieldy parts of myself, left those to the junkyard dogs to fight over.

The little violence is insidious because it makes me wonder whether it happened at all. Or whether I was making it up. Maybe I took it the wrong way. Maybe he didn't mean it. It makes me wonder whether I am as crazy as he told me I was. It makes me question where the line is, whether it was violence, whether I had the right to be afraid of him and make him feel bad.

It was small enough to keep me close because I knew how good it would feel when it would stop; small enough that stopping felt possible. One day, I thought. I will be good enough not to bring this on myself. I didn't leave him because of any of this, amazingly enough. I stayed small and out of sight for so long.

How to Burn Your Life to the Ground

It started with a life that someone else tried to plan for me. Parts of it belong to me, but I realized one morning, in the cold and beige basement apartment that looks out on a garden I am not allowed to access, that I do not, in fact, even belong to myself, save for some scraps. There are some bits scratched out in the parts of the dirt no one else knows I'm trying to tend in my spare time. But I am trying to grow all of it in the shade.

Spanish anarchist Buenaventura Durruti said, "We are not in the least afraid of ruins. We are going to inherit the earth, there is not the slightest doubt about that." On my good days, I try to believe him. To remember that he is a part of me. That I carry his heart and what he fought for in my back pocket.

I spend my days writing poetry on MUNI through San Francisco, from the Haight to the Sunset and back again. I barely study for the LSAT practice tests. I do well anyway. But I am clear with myself that anyone who is truly serious about burning a life to the ground will not, under any circumstances, actually go to law school.

That is life-building after all. It can provide kindling, but not the spark that is necessary to actually ignite a life that was well-intentioned and designed to please. It is too tidy.

I leave my partner alone for too long. I am too smart for him. I also, simultaneously, fail to live up to my potential. Burning your life to the ground involves drinking seriously, taking drugs effusively, and fucking around even though you are old enough to know better. I permit myself to be carelessly adrift in a world that seems to demand that I am palatable and ambitious but also filled with self-hatred. I allow myself to falter.

Here's how to do it, if you want to follow my blueprint.

Go to Canada, first of all.

Wait.

First major in poetry: that is what tilts the logs toward one another. It provides the pages that will ignite first and offer the dry warmth so that the rest of it goes up. Make grilled cheese in your apartment after the bar closes and dance around your apartment with the vaulted ceilings.

Then, go to Canada. Do not come home until you're deported, until you're dragged kicking and screaming. Until you've learned enough that you can't unsee how untenable and ridiculous your little life is.

Maybe it will take you time to see what you need to burn; it took me years too long. I didn't recognize the broken clock at first or the repetitive fights that demeaned the dreams I had that were my own.

Maybe it will take you time to gather the materials to make a proper fire of it. Without the proper materials, you'll just be burning holes in the soles of your shoes with your cigarettes. Maybe you'll just be walking out to the end of your block for a smoke until you die, trying to hide the tar under your fingernails and letting that suffice for ignition.

To really burn your life to the ground, you have to let it engulf you. Only then will it split the seed of who you are meant to be wide open. You need to let it break your heart, to ruin you, until you're pacing the halls in the middle of the night, relearning how to move the human body in which you find yourself.

Eventually, I settled in among the ashes of what I had destroyed. Sifted through the rubble for a broken toy or a discarded baby tooth, left behind by my powerful imagination. I took stock of what did not burn. Noticed who brought a meal when I was standing in the hollow shell of my kitchen. Once the flames were gone, I had to relearn how to feed myself amidst the unmistakable charred smell. I would wake up late and dry my tears on the hardwood floor of an apartment I discovered belongs entirely to me. My own scrap of borrowed real estate. I relished the thought that there was no going back to the predestined life.

I was no longer afraid of ruins. I had walked through the ruins of my own making and survived.

I vowed to belong to myself. I ignored that it would take years to recognize my life. But one day, I want to tell myself, you will walk into a room and all eyes will be on you. People will tug at your sleeve to ask you questions and share their fretting. You will be the one facilitating the meeting the night before the action, and you will be the one with the plan everyone shuts the fuck up to hear. Listen, you could hear a pin drop, I want to tell that sad self.

They will take the legal support form seriously. They will believe you when you say that they are safe. You will tell them where the bathrooms are, how to locate the exits in the event of an emergency. You will inhabit your body in a way that does not command, but whispers. You will hear the sigh of relief on the other end of the line when a friend recognizes that you're a capable nerd. That you've already played the scenario to the end three times in the shower this morning.

I do not remember the moment when this happened. I did not look back. But I am certain that it started with a match. Or it could have, I'm not sure. Everything that matters about me is still here.

Bumping Into Walls

When I returned home from Canada, I missed the loon song and spent my days wandering through Golden Gate Park, looking for the darkest, most silent space. If I could not have the people I left behind, I wanted enough solitude to speak to them, my imaginary friends. I longed for the wind on the boat and to feel the thrill of an eagle slicing the sky, returning to its nest, and the delight of falling asleep on the ground after a day of moving my body through the open world, without any walls at all.

I wanted to unmake everything. I cried once. Then I put an end to a love that was really just a heap of scraps to sift through, which he treated as a gift. Here. This is what I have to offer. This is what you are worth. Instead, I plunged a dagger through its heart, putting an end to its suffering. It was nothing but smoldering wreckage that I mistook for heat. I decided that I could not make a life without passion. I decided that I was unwilling to continue starving myself to death wandering through the wilderness after a love just out of reach.

I moved into a studio apartment, bought a busted bicycle, and filled myself with avocados, cheap at the Mexican produce market around the corner. I dared to take up space by feeding myself whatever I wanted. I ordered the combo at Boogaloos every time: refusing to choose between eggs and pancakes. On the weekends, I would buy a bag of donuts from the Chinese donut shop at 18th and Mission, vanilla with rainbow sprinkles, and eat them in the quiet of my apartment which was mine in its entirety. After dinner, I would walk to the collectively-owned bookstore, open until 9pm. I would wander through the aisles and buy woodcut print posters for my apartment or queer history or books about the ecology of places I longed to go and even more longed to protect. No matter how many destinations I created for myself beyond the studio on South Van Ness, I kept bumping into its walls.

There was a corner where I would catch my right shoulder, like a stranger hurrying to the train. There was a spot in the kitchen that would reach out and grab my left elbow. I stubbed my toe on the lip between the hallway and the bathroom, the one with tiny tiles and a clouded window overlooking the alley. The one where I had an entire built-in cabinet for my things: for the makeup and potions that felt necessary now that I had a mirror again. The ones I could do without when the lake was the only thing to wipe me clean.

To walk out the front door, you more or less had to walk into the bathroom, then open the door, out into the sterile hallway where the kids who lived on the floor would play kickball on Saturday mornings. I started wearing skinny jeans. I bought rain boots I still have.

Once, someone high on meth tried to break into my apartment in the middle of the night, shimmying down the fire escape. There's nothing here for you, I wanted to say. There's nothing here worth having.

Blur

When I think of the Ford action, I think of myself sitting in the passenger seat on the drive home from the Ford dealership with my feet up on the dashboard, listening to Iron and Wine while Mike from Canada gives me segments of pomelo—pale and sweet—and his sweatshirt for the air conditioning we can't figure out how to turn down.

We pulled into the Greenpeace warehouse—when it was still in the city—in the dark. In my mind, we unload the chains, although when I look at the pictures, I'm pretty sure that our people locked themselves to the chain already in front of the dealership.

So I must be imagining unloading a different chain that did not belong to Ford (and also did not get confiscated by police). And now I am wondering whether we got our U-Locks back from the Ford action—the ones we used to lock necks to the chain already at the Ford station.

When I work to remember the drive home, I remember that Mike and I were actually driving back from Sacramento in 2007, from a balloon banner action at the state building in Sacramento, urging the governor of California to create stricter emission standards, which did not happen. (Arnold Schwarrzenegger had his conveniently-timed epiphany about the climate crisis only after he left office.) And I'm wondering whether there were chains at that action.

The actions blur together after a while, but the feeling is the same. All of the equipment, a tangle. The demand sets begin to blend together. The faces change over the years, but the people, though, remain distinct. The tone of the experience is like a bell, clear and even. And the accumulation of experience in my body is sedimentary.

I am thinking about violence.

Once, in a yoga workshop, a teacher was discussing the philosophical underpinnings of violence and non-violence and stoicism—opining about the wisdom of the text, written down by a man who had lived all his life in an ashram, taught by someone who had also lived his whole life in an ashram. She had a warmth but no softness, an affection for the text but not the students in front of her. The onus is on you, the swami explained. If you are non-violent, then no violence can befall you. My heart crumpled, my face flushed, thinking of all the times I had received what she clearly believed I deserved. My hands shook taking notes, disbelieving what I transcribed.

I am thinking about fluency and expertise and intimacy, all shades of the same color.

I am thinking about tear gas and the way rubber bullets ricochet off asphalt on hot July nights. I am thinking about the way flashbangs light up the dark streets, the taste of the bandana that cannot save me from my poisoned snot. I am thinking about mutual aid, how we stick together, we do not run. We do not panic when they tell us to. I am thinking about the violence of a green carpet in an ashram with an altar adorned with rose petals, the cropped-hair nun who has never seen such things.

I am thinking about the necessity for the most granular specificity that reveals a larger truth. This is not chicken or egg, acorns exploding into forests. I cannot accept a larger truth built without foundation or cause if you want me to see you as anything other than a charlatan, a realtor of fantasy.

I raise a shaking hand. I do not make eye contact. I ask my teacher about violence. She tries to answer my question by repeating the text: *Broadly, generally, this is true, she points to the page, so it must also be true, specifically,* she seems to say. *Violence is bad.*

She is proud of this insight.

I am thinking about the cops who attacked a mother holding her baby. How they both had names. I am thinking about how they are not theoretical but visceral. How their faces moved and flesh shook. I am thinking about the mother's eyes as she took my camera so pictures could make it out. Seconds later, I was arrested, dragged to the police van. I can remember the songs we sang as they loaded us into a steel box. I remember the asphalt under my bare feet after they took my shoes away.

They must have had violence in their hearts. She tries to make the people fictional. She says "they" but means me. She cannot fathom risk or the guttural cries of a baby afraid of losing her mother. This nun has not set foot on a clearcut, which is violence, too.

I wonder, years later, if she believed the trees had violence in their hearts. If the land did, or the river, or the muskrat, or the stalks of wild rice, all poisoned with mercury. Whether the sky did, or the birds.

They attacked that mother for standing on a bridge, which, according to treaty law, belongs to her more than it belongs to anyone else. I am thinking about how the English may have built it, but it is built on unceded land. How it might as well have been built on clouds: an etheric thing with matter and volume but without a reasonable claim. I wonder whether the nun believes theft is violence. I wonder what she considers theft.

I am writing the stories I do not tell at parties. Buzzkill, doorway darkener, killjoy, good-time-ruiner. It sounds like "you had to be there" and feels like strange looks. There are memories I only replay to excavate something larger beneath the surface. It is no use trying to pick it apart from a distance; I have to squish it between my fingers. I choose to get close, intimate, sticky.

I cradle it to my face to know before I know what it will really mean. Even then, I do not share these thoughts freely.

I am thinking about Durga on the mantelpiece, resplendent with her necklace of skulls. I am thinking about her tiger's teeth. I am thinking about her blade.

A Small Stone

In my former life, I used to be cool. Which is to say, I went hiking a lot.

On the sign entering the trail, there were the usual admonishments to clean up after yourself and not to ride motorized vehicles. On a separate sign was a warning that, in great detail, explained what to do if one encountered a coyote. Finally, after all other options had been exhausted, the sign explained: YOU MAY THROW A SMALL STONE.

What will this do?

I do not ask. I imagine, and it is comical.

You are permitted to throw a small stone at the animal that is, according to myth, designed to outwit you—as though this is a generous blessing. A small stone is no match for a resident of the spirit world, renowned for its trickster nature, its cunning, its camouflage.

We deploy, "You may throw a small stone" as a sardonic offering: you are absolutely fucked, but here. You may throw a small stone. Good luck with that. Thoughts and prayers and godspeed to you. It will not help, yet we count this as charity. You get your first small stone for free. This sarcastic password is not meant to be comforting, but rather an artifact of our past life, when we were cool.

I never saw a coyote on that trail. I have never had cause to throw a stone. I have never reached into the cool dawn of my pocket for something to scare away the wild.

One night, in the kitchen, I am eating raw cookie dough with my hands, pinching it between my fingers, and my husband asks, "Were you raised by wolves?" My eyes shine and I smile my trickster grin, daring him. "You may throw a small stone," I laugh, like he has one hidden behind his back. And then we both laugh: like the feral beings that still live in our ribs.

Not Legal Advice

This is not legal advice. I am not an attorney. (I am definitely not your attorney.) This is not legal advice, and your mileage may vary.

Do not talk to cops. Do not give them any unnecessary advice or answer any unnecessary questions, even if they seem benign. Even if you think you aren't doing anything wrong. Even if they seem nice. Even if they tell you that your friends already talked. Even if you just want to clarify, if only you could explain, if only you could make them understand. Even, even, even.

I'm telling you a joke: *How can you tell when a cop is lying to you?*

The punchline: *They're talking!* We laugh, because it's true. (Then we stop laughing, because it's true.)

Do tell a cop who has arrested you before, who has a kind face, despite the fact that he has been trained to lie to you, despite the fact that you are not to speak to him, that you are pregnant so that, just in case, maybe he won't drop you on your face while you're in handcuffs. Tell him this, and watch his face congratulate you. Tell him this for protection—not to make conversation or to receive those congratulations. You say this, not for yourself. But for everything that stirs inside you, for everything in you that yearns for a future. When we say we are doing it for future generations, we mean it.

And then, after you and your friends have your arrest citations in hand, the cops thank you all for being so cooperative and professional. You and your friends will talk about this for years to come. How odd it was. How it may have restored your faith in humanity. (Just a little bit. Against your better judgment.) But ACAB, y'know. Because we haven't gone soft and forgotten our history over one small kindness and act of dignity.

The window did not feel pain when it was shattered into a spider web, cracking under the pressure of a brick, which also did not feel pain. And yet, the cops will avenge these symbols more readily than they would a child's life. They will ascribe pain and meaning and intention and fucking symbolism to it. They will make false equivalencies and fashion straw men and demand obedience. They will not come to save you. They cannot protect you because that is not how this country's history fashioned them.

Do not talk to the cops because maybe one day it will take two of them to arrest you and if you are feeling cheeky, you might ask them whether it makes them feel like big strong men that it takes two of them to arrest one of you. You are 110 pounds soaking wet after a summer of lawbreaking recklessness and chopping wood. They are decidedly not. Do not talk to the cops because if you ask them whether it makes them feel like big strong men, they might (because they are big strong men) then dislocate your shoulder. Do not talk to the cops because range of motion is nice to have and because if you talk to the cops, it will hurt when it rains.

(And because, *my god*, you think, *aren't I lucky, really*. It could have been so much worse.)

Arrestee Support Form

Please fill out this form so that, if you are arrested at the upcoming protest, we are able to track you through the legal system. For security purposes, this form will be shredded if you are not arrested, or once you have obtained legal counsel after your arrest.

Full Name: There is a name that lives in documents, but the names that live on the tongues of my beloveds are the ones that make me feel the fullest: Mama, Love, Sweetheart, Beautiful. Every voicemail from my father begins with, "Hey, Cutie, it's Dad." You can put that down, too.

Nickname/Preferred Name: Christy, Chris, Crust, CTS. Placed like medals around my neck in exchange for loyalty. Sanctified by familiarity. A shortened way to say, "Hey you!" but in a way that also says, "I love you and I see you. And I will name you my own way because what you mean to me is unique from what you mean to the state."

Date of Birth: A Sagittarius stellium means that I was born to run. That I wield a sword against illusion and injustice. Two months after I was born, my father had to trudge for miles in knee-deep snow to find medicine because I was burning up with fever; so much fire in me I nearly burned the house down. The stellium is in the seventh house, which means home and family. An astrologer once asked me how this takes shape in my life. My husband and I are both anarchists, I shrug. And this makes sense to her.

Home Address: Here, in this moment. Again and again.

Mailing Address: The house with the stained glass light over the front porch with a laurel leaf. The house where wisteria grows wild, shaking out its purple curls. You will know it by the mechanical winding sound the hummingbird makes as she sips from the red bell flowers in the front yard.

Your Contact Information: If you need to be in touch, leave a small piece of quartz by the edge of the garden or ask one of the neighborhood cats to call out to me. They know how to get my attention.

Emergency Contact: Dan will know what to do.

Contact Information: You can reach him by wafting the scent of coffee in his direction, or by digging your elbow into his right trapezius muscle. It has been so tense lately, and I worry.

Any medication you need/pertinent medical information?: The list is long, but I remember this: There was the time I sat at Pop's Bar and confessed that perhaps I was having a nervous breakdown after getting out of jail for the third—fourth?—time. I could explain how things need to be dark and warm for me to sleep and how drafty and loud and bright jail can be. But I could also tell you about the time I sang in jail out of boredom, and the next day the person in the cell next to mine thanked me for reminding her that she wasn't alone. And isn't that also medicine?

Any other information the legal support team should know if you are arrested?: There are cats to be fed and lunches to be made. There is a runny nose to be wiped and songs to be sung. There are bedcovers to be tidied and hair to be swept from his forehead. There is a cat who longs to curl herself against a ribcage which will not be there for her, and a child who will not understand if I do not make it home. A child who will count the days on his calendar, the one full of ships and endless seas.

If I'm being honest

Once, as a forest campaigner, I was in a meeting with a senior vice president for a company you've almost certainly heard of, who, because he mistook me for being my boss's intern, tried to convince me that I was making the perfect the enemy of the good (to which I replied that I didn't need to do that because he was already making the bad the enemy of the good) and, when I asked him whether he was including forest carbon in his company's emissions accounting, he said no and I asked why not, he replied—deftly, with an uncanny twinkle in his eye, like he'd done this before:

"Those numbers don't make things look too good," and he lowered his voice to add, "If I'm being honest."

I Sleep Just Fine

Somewhere, in some town, in some bar at some happy hour, or in the quiet of someone's home at a table full of roast chicken and salad, someone is telling the story of my villainy. A missed work meeting, a train made late with lockbox delays, a harshly worded letter that made them cry at their desk on a Tuesday, a long hoped-for promotion that never came to be. Perhaps that someone is the woman who was crying one day outside the bank lobby we were blockading, the bank where she worked in sustainability, and she sobbed that she had thought she was on the right side.

And I, playing my part in the story, am the nameless, faceless, anonymized villain at the center. It is a tender, reverent decision to ruin someone's day, week, career. Which is not to say it doesn't get easier. It gets more fluid all the time. The threats, the insults, the stories of my villainy feel farther away, as I move closer to the root of my convictions.

I think about the day my boss took me to a corporate meeting, and explained patiently to a Senior Vice President that while I resemble not so much a threat as a Pollyanna-shaped baked good, I am the one who could make his life a living hell—that while I was raised to appease, that is not my life's skill set. It was a compliment and I glowed in its light. And the senior vice president asked me how I sleep at night making trouble and ruining lives.

I did not set out to be the villain any more than I set out to be the hero. I move from love, and the rest is logistics.

But the logistics, it turns out, are my zone of particular genius. Counting steps from the door to the elevator bank. Timing deployment of our crew into an intersection in mere seconds. Practicing the flow of an action until we can't do it wrong.

Am I the hero today? Or the villain? Or both or neither? I cannot decide how I am interpreted. I am entitled to my own actions and efforts and reasoning and nothing more. But after rallying in the street with banners that take up two lanes of traffic or linking arms in front of corporate offices or blockading an oil refinery or a logging road, I have to go home to look at myself in the mirror and sleep inside the truth of my own conscience just like everyone else.

And when I pull the stars across my eyelids; when my cat holds my hand in her paws in the dark, like a mother she'd long forgotten; when my breathing slows to the frog song or the round hoots of the Great Horned Owl on the wind, I remember my place as a tiny bioluminescent organism riding the tide of the universe itself. In those moments, hot with my own pulse, bright with the possibility of a new world, I sleep just fine.

The Unfinished Protest

You get pinched before you make it to the door. The car following you wasn't all in your head. They really are out to get you. The bank shuts itself down before you can slam it closed. The cops beat you at your own game and blockade the entrance before you can get in place. There is something tragic in an unfinished protest.

To blockade a building, you could stand shoulder to shoulder or could link arms or legs. But I prefer a lockbox. It is appropriately intimidating especially if you have, as I do at first glance, the badass quotient of a blueberry muffin. It is also strong enough to withstand someone trying to break your arm. (Or so I've heard.)

Begin with a pvc tube. (Perhaps you want something stronger, like steel, but unless you have a strong welding background, I recommend starting with the pvc.) Test it to make sure you can get your arm inside. If you'll be outside, make sure you can fit your arm inside while wearing a raincoat. Drill two holes in the round tube halfway between the two cut edges, straight through. Screw a bolt through the two holes, and secure the bolt with duct tape (to hold it in place and make sure that no one snags themselves on the bolt). Stick your arm in the tube and grab onto the pin. The edge of the tube should rest in the crook of your elbow. Now, cover the box in white painters tape and write your message on the tube: Climate Justice Now! NO on SB 1080! (Your mileage may vary.)

The unfinished protest will always have a whisper of what might have been: a crime interrupted. It will become the anecdote you will use in trainings to illustrate your point. A hard-won lesson.

So you try not to get pinched.

Sometimes they're trying to pull your arm out of the lockbox before you've even had a chance to sit down. The quickest blockade deployment I've ever done was eight seconds. The security guard didn't even make it out from behind the desk. To actually lock yourself into the lockbox, you'll need two carabiners and two smallish lengths of cord, knotted into a circle and tied to the carabiner. Loop the cord around your wrist, stick your arm into the lockbox and clip the carabiner to the pin in the middle of the box.

How do they get you out of the box? Like a magic trick; they think they know the secret. The jaws of life. An angle grinder. But then, at the last minute, Ah! You find the trick to the puzzle box. You unclip before the grinder meets flesh.

Sometimes, they don't know what's coming. People in San Francisco know too much. Everyone is, perhaps, a little too prepared. So if you want to buy yourself a little distraction, fill the lockbox with flowers. And decorate it with gift wrap. It will look like a bouquet. At the last moment, rip the paper and cast the flowers to the marble floor of the lobby. As you sit for hours, you will feel like a celebrated diva as the flowers slowly wilt.

At one Wells Fargo shareholder meeting, we never got to unwrap our bouquets. We never locked down. We never had to unclip or turn around to have plastic cuffs applied. Never had to be fingerprinted or sign a citation. There is something empty about an unfinished protest. But we all went for lunch afterward anyway, stealing fries from each others' plates.

How to Build a Concrete Barrel

Building a concrete barrel is probably really easy. I wouldn't know, I've never done it. What I'm guessing is that you can find most of the materials you'd need at your local hardware store. Oil barrels are easy enough to come by if you know where to look.

To know how to build a concrete barrel, you will first know how to build a lockbox. I've provided brief instructions in the previous essay (see the essay, "The Unfinished Protest") for how I'm guessing you might build a lockbox which—on the advice of counsel—I want to be very clear I have never done, to my recollection.

To build one concrete lockbox barrel, you should first build one lockbox.

Next, procure a 42 gallon oil drum. Clean the outside. The inside doesn't matter, as it will be filled with concrete. Simply ensure that the inside has nothing that will clog up your Sawzall (see next step).

Stand the barrel upright and use a Sawzall to cut two round holes on opposing sides of the barrel. The holes should be slightly larger than the circumference of your lockbox and at about elbow height of the person locking down (when they are seated with their arm extended inside the lockbox). Take your time figuring out where to put the holes as this is the position in which a person will (theoretically, of course) be spending several hours. To make them more comfortable, you might put a foam pad underneath their seat. Just in case the ground is cold. (I don't know; sometimes the ground is cold.)

Place the lockbox through the two holes in the barrel and secure it with gorilla glue and duct tape.

Purchase your Quikrete. You'll need somewhere between 280 and 350 pounds of Quikrete to fill the barrel. (Note: This is not an exact science and I'm just guessing here.)

Either way, it will be heavy enough that once it's in place, it will be hard as hell to move, which is the point. No need to quibble too strongly about math here—I've done some basic geometry for you.

Next, mix the concrete. I hear that some people mix it in a metal wheelbarrow. Try mixing twenty to forty pounds at a time with water. Mix with a metal shovel. Once well-mixed, pour the mix into the barrel and prepare the next batch. Don't mix too much at a time, as you will have to lift that wheelbarrow to pour.

You'll probably want a day or so to let it cure completely. It might be faster than that, but again, I wouldn't know.

Attach your messaging to the outside of the barrel. Something quippy like STOP FUNDING THE CLIMATE CRISIS or BILLIONAIRES ARE A POLICY FAILURE. Your mileage may vary.

You could, theoretically, use this concrete barrel to reinforce any kind of a blockade: railways, entrances to oil refineries, logging roads, corporate headquarters. They are heavy as fuck and may be hard to deploy, but they are probably incredibly hard to remove and frustrating for law enforcement and your target. In my experience, fire fighters generally have better toys and will be called in to drill you out, should you choose not to walk away willingly.

I mean, if you're into that kind of thing. I wouldn't have any experience with that to draw from.

On Intimacy

There is intimacy, and then there is this: *Take off all your clothes on the porch.*

He stands in the doorway, light streaming from behind him. I want him to hold me, to press my cells together and make me whole. He does not touch me, but takes my phone and keys. It's alright, he says. Gingerly, he puts my clothes in the washing machine, as I briefly dress in his sweatpants. We try not to wake our sleeping child: we do not stand over his small bed to marvel at his curls tonight. I do not dare kiss his sweaty cheek. I do not want my poisoned rebellion to tarnish him.

My love speaks in whispers, and I barely speak at all. There is fluency in glances. We know what to do. Home is a miracle, even if safety is an illusion. The quiet cushions me.

He runs the shower and I wash the tear gas out of my hair. I scrub it from behind my ears, from under my shabby fingernails, from the places it couldn't have reached. I slough the shouting from my skin.

Don't run. Don't talk to the cops. Remember: you didn't see a thing.

The inside of my brain is bright with flashbangs, the reflections off their helmets. I let the water run hot across my body, bracing myself against the wall. I let the water shake the sound from my cells. Against the cold tile, I still feel the helicopter blades slicing the sky. I feel the hum of screaming asphalt.

Our years together are a series of small intimacies like this.

In fifteen years, he has been late for dinner exactly once: he was on a bus headed to jail. My friends told me not to worry. Their boyfriends would rather be late than in jail. But I called the hotline and yes: kettled and arrested, they said. He spent half the night on a bus and I spent the following day eating barbecue tofu outside the concrete tower, waiting for my beloved's face among the newly liberated. Buried my face into his jacket when I finally held him. I told him not to leave me again, knowing that, too often, I am the one to leave.

Take off all your clothes on the porch means: We can turn back the night.

we can wash it all clean. It means, you are home and here, and so am I. It is the possibility of starting again in the morning, the promise of a hot cup of coffee and whispers and furtive glances. It is the shorthand of the plan that is always in place.

One night, we took the freeway, dancing with our friends like we were free. I could see his face, illuminated by flash bangs. Smoke clung to our clothes. An electric kind of espionage: sneaking into a future where the highways belong to people. Where every beloved's prison door opens and their hearts pour into the street with us.

I come to bed and he holds my spine against his beating heart.

Store-Bought is Fine

1. The fake prelit Christmas tree in my attic, waiting for the day after Thanksgiving when it will be assembled and bring small joy for a season, without having to deal with pine needles everywhere and the cutting down of a tree that should have lived.

2. The serotonin, or rather: the SSRIs that allow me to mostly sleep through the night, that allow me to mostly appear to be a functioning person who does the things she is supposed to be doing, and which even sometimes allow me not to catastrophize about the end of the world, about the polar bears and the floods and the fires and the drought which will eliminate our food and the overfishing and the carbon trading schemes that will only make the rich more powerful.

3. The pumpkin bread baked at home but made from a store-bought mix from which my child still manages to feel loved and cared for. And which, while scraping its crumbs from his plate, will cause my child to utter the words, "You're the best mama." Which is not true, I am certain of it, but feels true to my child at that moment. So I do not correct him. Who am I to say?

4. The things I could have made, but didn't.

5. Or didn't want to.

6. Or didn't have the time.

7. Or didn't have the emotional wherewithal to endure making from scratch.

8. The way I look at social media and all the homemade crafts and food and clothing and lives that other mothers make the time to perform

and I simply cannot summon the energy or courage or serotonin to give a shit about. The things I can't bear to use my creativity to bring to life, as I am far too busy keeping myself alive.

9. The way I don't berate myself for showing up late for things when it doesn't matter. The way I celebrate having made it to the party at all. The way my arms are full of store-bought love, but no one notices and even if they did, they're just glad we're still here.

The Sellout

Like most humans, I am wrong a lot.

Since becoming a parent, I have become more careful in my wrongness. Admitting it quickly, apologizing profusely, making fewer promises than I would like to, because I would like to make all the promises, but I only make the ones I know that I can keep; I would like to promise the world; I would like to promise it will all be okay; I would like to promise beauty and hope and belonging in every facet of every moment. But I would like it to be more than a promise: I would like to contain the world in my outstretched hands and say, here.

Nonchalantly, no big deal, just ran to the store while you were at school to bring you every treasure that existence itself has to offer like I'm pulling a popsicle from the freezer. A popsicle is a promise I know that I can keep—because I put them there myself—and so I do.

But I am wrong a lot. And sometimes I lie without knowing that I am lying.

When I was pregnant and fascists were marching through the streets and I asked my obstetrician what she knew about the effects of tear gas on pregnant bodies and she shrugged and said something goofy about not knowing if there was science on that yet, and we were all terrified, I had to give a speech. It was not the speech itself that was the problem. The problem was that I gave a speech about climate justice to a group of high school and college students and I lied to them.

Inadvertently, but all the same.

Standing in the stuffy auditorium behind a battered podium with my gray maternity dress pulled around new geography, I began the speech telling them that I had no special words of wisdom, that I did not know what to say, but that I was prepared to fight, and that was true. And I told them that I was prepared to put my body and my freedom on the line for our future and that was true.

The part where I lied was the part where someone asked me how having a baby had changed how I viewed climate activism, and I said, "It hasn't."

Because I did not know what I would be prepared to do once I saw his full moon of a face, his eyes like treasures from a recovered shipwreck, damp and beautiful.

And I knew then that I was wrong. That I had lied. I would sell any of you out in a heartbeat for him.

I guess what I'm saying is that it's a good thing that our liberation is bound up in one another's. His and yours and mine and ours. I did not lie when I said I would fight.

Make Sure.

I love the way my child says make sure-ing, rather than making sure. I'm make sure-ing of you, mama. He tells me not to laugh. Remember, this is important.

I love the way the cat's paw rests on my hand in bed, in the dark, in the soft space between now and sleep. She is making sure of me. Or make sure-ing. What is the word for certainty in cat? But when she is satisfied, she sighs, and that is the signal that I can move my hand somewhere else. Underneath the covers or my cheek. It does not matter to her. She is sure.

I am sure of very little. I am reading the results of a kidney ultrasound, comparing numbers to the normal range. I am reading through the recipe. I am giving my phone number to the man in the shop. But this does not amount to certainty.

I love the sharp geometry of a hummingbird's beak, its mechanical winding sound, its tongue like lightning. There was an orange one outside the dining room window last week and I had to open the book to find out what it was. Skimming for the orange color in pages darting past, the way it swam through the leaves of the bottlebrush tree. I was sure I saw it. I was sure it was orange. Yes, it was a hummingbird. I'm telling you.

There are only so many qualifiers I can eliminate before I sound like a robot, a mouth without a person. Because I am not sure at all, is what I'm saying. I am winging it all the time. I am adding ginger where none is called for. I am peering at the numbers through my reading glasses. I am slipping feet into shoes, trusting that they will carry me. Time is flying, and I am hanging onto the rudder. I am telling you what I remember, knowing that at least half of it is a lie.

I love the way the loon's songs skip across the lake at daybreak. I love the moment the water reaches my scalp: cold, animating my hair into its own organism, brackish, dark. I love the way the ladybugs curl up inside of hollow logs by the thousands. I love the quiet of my own breath, standing still as we watch the fox flick its tail at dusk. I take my son's hand: there, look. His face looks up at me for certainty.

Mirror/translator.

I hold open my hands. This is how the world is. I point. I am the moon.

This does not mean I can understand the world, that I have the words for it. Like this. Not exactly this. I apologize. I admit that I am wrong.

I love the way the music sounds when you sing it, bouncing off the walls of the kitchen and the rice on the stove. The way you say, let's run. The way my heart skips a beat when I see a cement mixer. You understand? It's not about the cement. There is something in the hum of the engine. Even when you are not there, I want to grab your hand and say, look!

There is something in the dirt to love. Not just your fingers, but the worms, the seeds. They are going about their business. They are trying their best and it is heartbreaking. They do not know any better than I.

There was a caterpillar, once. As long as my index finger and as round, electric yellow. Surreal and artificial, and yet there it was. That was a long time ago, on a different coast. I don't know their names. I didn't forget. I never knew. There were things I did know once that then dissolved while I was sleeping or kissing his sweaty forehead in his sleep, peppery and sweet. That loosened their grip on me as the cat twitched from dreaming.

I do not tell him about the times I almost died. I do not say what I would do on his behalf. What is the use? The enormity of my love would terrify him, to think that such a thing is necessary, that there is a world so haunting and viscous that it would require a love like this, ready to bear its teeth. I let him eat his oatmeal before we fling the door open, tender in the face of a world like this. I don't know how we endure it.

Instead, I think about the temporary pleasures of a body. The euphoria of a bandana askew. The way the pasta bites back. My feet against the porch railing. My own knees, my god. Can you imagine?

I do not know how to explain the world. My child asks about tomorrow, and I promise it. He says it Tomollow, round and plump. It lilts at the end, always a question. It has to do with hot chocolate or riding bicycles or a new book, you see? Tomorrow, tomorrow. I do not deny him the promise of it. All the proof so far tells me that it is true.

Yes, tomorrow.

But I am not sure of much, even these fragile promises. There is horror and beauty that I find inexplicable. What I remember clearly is the curve of a cup, the weight of it, the way the sugar sinks to the bottom. The way the backs of my legs stick to the vinyl booth. You are human, do you remember? At once here, in this moment, eating pancakes. The next: unstuck, I am walking out into the morning. I look at the sky, make sure-ing.

HELLO!

We—my child and I—invented a game that is simply this: shouting "HELLO!," into each other's mouths loudly, over and over again—seeking each other out through aggressive echolocation, shouting into the soles of each other's feet, vibrating with being found. We collapse into reams of laughter that last longer than the game, "HELLO!" ricochets off every one of my cells, a laughing meditation in which the world fades into a void of white and we are gasping for breath and I look into his face and remember that he will not always be three.

Hello, I see you.

Hello, I love you.

Hello, I am here and you are here and we are here together and it's such a miracle, isn't it.

It's such a miracle, *hellohellohello*.

Pretend Your Foot is a House

My child tells me, Pretend your foot is a house so I can safely live there.

My foot becomes a house. We crawl inside. I lay out carpets and push the furniture against the arch of my foot so we can have dance parties and eat pizza on the floor. Against its pronating edge, I hang his school art projects on the refrigerator. He goes to sleep in my pinky toe, and I flip the pillow over to the cool side for him. He snores gently and I pull the covers around his chin. The moonlight streams in through the toenail. I close the curtains and turn out the light. From my room in the big toe, I can hear him breathing. The cats chase a mouse across my instep in the darkness. My ankle remembers what he forgets. I hang lights in its vaulted ceiling, illuminating a gothic tower that holds our history. Flying buttresses spring outward from my bones to cradle us both, to steady us against uncertainty. When it is cold, the joists shift and creak. We patch over the places where the light gets in. We dry our socks in the fireplace of my heel.

The last night he lived inside my body, I walked through the house—the real house, which is not my foot—in the dark and the silence. My feet—where he wishes to safely live—against the wood floors, soles unfurling against the cool trees.

You have always safely lived here, I say.

All That Matters

Today, my son wears his motorcycle tee shirt to school with teal pants and a blue backpack with cars and trucks all over it and red socks with flamingos. Standing at the counter, I carefully pack his lunch bag. The one with mermaids, so he and his best friend can have matching lunch bags. I velcro his brown shoes extra tight, I adjust his green mask. I pinch it to his nose and squinch my face and we both laugh. I smooth his hair with its perfect and plentiful cowlicks, and he bats my hand away. I would pull him back inside my skin if I could.

I memorize this in case I need to tell you later.

Like I've memorized his laugh and the way his hair smells when he's still dreamy and sticky from a nap. Like I've memorized a thousand things: his hand in mine and the cowrie shell curve of his ear. The weight of his body against mine when it's windy like it was this morning and his muscles tense against it and the little sound he makes to ward off the chill. The way he holds his stuffed fox to his face when he sleeps. The way you need to hold a washcloth over his eyes when you wash his hair.

Do you understand? They won't be able to ask me about those things, so I have to memorize his motorcycle tee shirt.

He probably wanted the one with the bulldozer, but it was in the laundry. This is what we do to pretend things are normal, to build a façade of okay-ness. We do the laundry, we eat oatmeal for breakfast, we pack lunches and make lists and smooth cowlicks and buy soap. We celebrate birthdays with little red velvet cupcakes and trips to the museum. I nurse sick-days with blue Pedialyte and penguin videos and a new coloring book.

I do all the things I was told. We pretend everything is promised.

Inside the mermaid lunch bag is his bento box. He would want me to tell you what's inside today.

Leftover sweet potato fries and rice and paneer and watermelon for dessert, and his favorite spoon, and his brand new fire truck water bottle. I cradle the bento with his favorite orange cloth napkin.

Every parent at school drop-off is hollow-eyed, every hug a bit too long, and our babies squirm out of our arms and into their classrooms where, my son tells me, he will be working on his letters today with his little chalkboard. Before he goes, I hug him and tell him I love him with my whole heart. I will be there to pick him up. I will be there.

I promised him after school today that he can eat his snacks in the car and we'll take the car to the drive-through car wash. So I pack the snacks and tuck them into my bag and he shrieks with delight as we drive through it. This weekend, he wants to go to the station and sit and watch the trains. These are the promises he asks me to make, and I make them readily, happily. He cannot fathom what other promises could be better than this. What could be better than keeping a promise to your child?

Better, but not simple—you see?

There are machinations in the world grinding against my promise-keeping that haunt my dreams. How precarious it all is: my promises and his tiny body. I am holding it together with both hands and most of my teeth, willing it to last.

There are promises—ones he cannot imagine. He cannot imagine the fear in what I cannot guarantee. I spent so long wishing him into the world, sharing my body, helping him open his eyes. Teaching him how to eat and dress himself and write his name. I have given over years to the kindness of ritual: the certainty of bedtime and the ease of each morning, following the same structure. My only goal is to become what I avoided for so long: safe and predictable and soft and cheerful and steadfast. I repeat myself. I beg him to brush his teeth.

One day, it will annoy or embarrass him that I say the same things over and over again. He will roll his eyes and sigh dramatically, and I will know I have been a mother because he will be able to recite my own love back to me. *I love you with my whole heart. You are so important to me. I hope you have an amazing day. What was the most fun part of school? I hope you have sweet dreams.*

I hope. I love. He does not see that I also rage and mourn and bargain and beg and twist my shirt in the school parking lot. I hold my face in my hands. I hold his heart in my memory, the first patter of knowing him.

I have been unwavering, but to what end?

So, I pack his lunch and straighten my face when he asks, "What's wrong, mama?" and camouflage my fear behind affection. I sit on the floor playing magnatiles, pretending I am not watching his face, memorizing his expressions, falling in love with the way his eyebrows furrow and the corner of his mouth moves.

I cannot tell him what I fear.

So, I do his laundry and hang his fire truck shirt in his closet and make his bed and hold his hand when we cross the street and bring the right snacks and remember sunscreen and make doctors' appointments and dutifully attend parent-teacher conferences. I pack his lunch box with his favorite things, holding a stone in my throat, as though packing his lunch with all his favorite things will matter.

Because it does matter.

Popsicles at the End of the World

The world is ending, so we are eating popsicles on the porch.

I am almost through with the day's horror when it is time to pick up my son at school. I smile, we hug, I tell him I missed him. And he asks me to eat popsicles on the porch. To which I say yes, because his inheritance is a burning thing, a grotesque tangle; I gesture, this will someday be yours.

In my child, the future is already here: the rain boots in the hall, which didn't get much use during what used to be "the rainy season"; the way we account for risk, which changes every day.

The daily work of climate grief is a heavy, heady slog. We heal, we open again: the daily work of keeping safe. I do not mention the peril of sending him to school. There is risk in being inside—intimacy and a pandemic, hand in hand—so his schools keep the windows open. But when the fires come, which they will again this season, what then? We shut the windows in the house and turn on the air purifiers. He sits by the window, staring through the haze and wondering when he can ride his bicycle again.

My chest tightens when I leave him on the porch by himself. What could happen? My anxiety glowers at me from under my skin, giving me thousands of answers. It clenches its teeth, because I ought to know already. The possibilities splinter, a fractal of devastation: too many children lost in an instant these days. Wait here, I say. Not because I don't trust him. But because there is creeping dread in letting him out of my sight. I think of the number of parents who did not know it was the last time they would see their children's faces. Inside, I move quickly. I gasp when I see his face when I open the door again.

I remember—the grief is enormous and his hands are so small. So this is what I do: say yes to popsicles to soothe the ache of a burning world. I put my feet up on the ledge of the porch and let his sweaty head press against my shoulder and watch the bees sip from the orange flowers in the front yard. Every bee, a blessing, an omen. A resistance against collapse and apathy.

The cold trail of juice runs down his arm and he shrieks. He pulls away and there is a shock of relief, the breeze cooling the part of my shoulder where his sticky scalp rested. Our T-shirts soaked through by closeness. I want to pull him back, in time, inward, here, again, more.

I say yes as often as I can. To videos and snuggles and books and just one more. Racing the daylight to the horizon, fitting as much of him into the day as I can. Wasting nothing. Carving every memory into the walls, marking his height on the doorframes. Another popsicle, another game, frantic for as much of it as I can stomach. We shut the shades and turn on the window air conditioner. This is, for now, our bubble against the shifting climate, a makeshift escape from the heat. We set out bowls of ice for the squirrels and count ourselves the luckiest: together, in the cool air, above the sea.

These are the days when time breaks my heart: a home being swept downriver; it will only become more common. The time will come when it won't matter anymore how deep we have sunk our roots.

What to Bring

Once again, this isn't legal advice. I was never here.

But if I were, I could hand you a little slip of paper, and it would read something like this. Here is what to bring with you. Here is what not to bring. Here is what will keep you safe. Here is what you must omit to keep your friends safe. These are the necessary things for a protest.

What to Bring
- A government-issued ID

- $20 or a transit card with enough money on it to get home.

- A chant-sheet, talking points,

- The legal hotline number written in sharpie somewhere (covered) on your body

- Any prescription drugs you will not be able to go without for 72 hours, should you be arrested. The medicine should be in its original prescription packaging with your name on it.

- Wear layers and sturdy, closed-toed shoes.

What Not to Bring
- Legal forms or any other paper with participants' identifying information.

- An unlocked phone or other device with contact information or plans. Please ensure the device is locked with a passcode, not touch/face ID.

- A weapon or anything that could be construed as a weapon.

- Any jewelry or other valuables.

- Contact lenses (wear glasses instead).

- Illicit drugs, including marijuana, even if you have a prescription for it.

And if I were giving you training in direct action, this is the list I would give you. Give or take. Your mileage may vary. As with everything else, I am not a lawyer. Please consult a lawyer with knowledge of your local laws.

My true advice is to bring the small stone your child gave you for luck. Place the slip in your back pocket, and worry it with your thumb when things get tense, so you may remember why you are here and why you need to make it home. Leave him with a lipstick kiss on the back of his hand he can wear all day: proof that you are with him and a promise that you are coming back.

Bring your grandmother's songs so you have something to comfort you (and the person in the next cell) in the middle of the night. To ward off the cold and boredom. To give your mind something to do besides spiral in a place they have designed to send you spinning. To remember that you cannot be alone when you are part of a lineage.

You should bring a full belly, since the food in jail is inedible, and it will give you more mass with which to plant yourself on the sidewalk and a sturdiness with which to lift your voice inside the atrium. And bring snacks to give peoples' mouths something to do besides talk to the cops.

Do not bring your fear of failure or your good-girl, people-pleasing, pick-me attitude. Bring your charming smile, but not your complacency or your agnostic wondering about whether this could possibly move the needle. It does because it must.

Bring your stories and your 6 a.m. laughter even when you would rather be in your cozy bed. Bring contingency plans and blankets and a first aid kit and an appreciation for the ones who kicked in the door so that you could stand here in the first place.

Bring your ancestors and your willingness to be an ancestor and the hope of every generation after you.

First Aid

At five, my child carries a first aid kit with him. On weekends, to the playground, on bicycle rides, to the grocery store. Just in case.

His teacher tells me at pickup that he was the first to her side when she cut her finger; to his friend's side when she dropped her glass and spilled her water; to the new child's side. "It's nice here," he tells her.

He carries his "emergency kit" with the confidence of someone who has fallen off the bicycle and gotten back on, whom I call brave whenever I can. He carries it with solemnity across his five year-old body and tells me, "Let's hope we never have to use it."

Perhaps Kate Chopin Had a Point

There are days in the life of a mother with depression that contain an eternity.

There are days when one might begin to think, perhaps Kate Chopin had a point. Kate Chopin, who wrote The Awakening, and was descended from three generations of women who were widowed young, and was the product of a Catholic education where she was expected to handle her own money, a startlingly radical notion at the time. The Awakening, in which Kate Chopin beckoned her most famous character, Edna Pontellier in The Awakening, to leave her family and assert her autonomy by simply walking into the sea. Edna Pontellier, who met her end in a gentle and stoic drowning, taken by flotsam and a green undertow.

Perhaps she had a point, I think.

And then my child says something devastating. Something like, *I love you unstoppable.*

Just for instance. It wouldn't have to be that, but something like that. And I think: *perhaps I will stay here on the shore.*

Waves

Every time my husband and child are five minutes late coming home from a bicycle ride because they stopped at (just one more!) Little Free Library, I am convinced that they have both died and my grief begins plotting itself against my life like waves lapping at the door, and then they come around the corner, my son squealing on the back of the bike, and I am released back into my own tangible—though only temporarily-certain—life.

High Priestess of the Apocalypse

If what we are dealing with is a simple rapture, then my work is straightforward. To dispose of the perishable food before it goes bad; to redistribute whatever will keep. To rehome the cats and the dogs bereft at the loss of owners who did not conceptualize a heaven that included them. And the ill-advised birds who were never going to make it there anyway. Watch the green one, she'll take your finger right off.

In this scenario, we will become the collective executors of our earthly inheritance. It will be a drudgery and a joy to dole out homes and cars and human rights once we are left to our own devices. Door to door: Who is still here? Who had enough fun to spare them from an early leaving? Who is left to delight in corporeality? It is brevity that makes it precious.

If it is zombies, we will board up the house for as long as we can. We survive on the soup and the preserves I painstakingly made from our garden, the planter boxes they will uproot with their soggy feet. The precious fruit trees we tended with the ladder they will also mangle.

From the outside, it does not look like I am well-equipped to fend off zombies. On my surface, I have the punk-rock credibility of a blueberry muffin. But watch: I heft 16-pound sledgehammer. I fill an oil barrel to the brim with concrete; this will weigh about 350 pounds. I know the weights of things, at the very least.

I wield a nail gun to board up the windows. One, two, three, four: each thwack an injury to the frame, a gaping hole in the curb appeal that used to matter when this was a home and not a last stand.

If the end of the world is an actual political revolution to prevent the end of the world, well, you have come to the right place. This one is the one I have trained for; the one I have trained others to expect. In this one, we will join in.

I will make molotov cocktails and put them in the backpack you used to wear to school: printed with trains and trucks. I will place them gently in your mermaid insulated lunch box so you may throw them with your tiny, ineffectual, five year-old arms. At cop cars, at government buildings. I will straighten your balaclava and tell you I'm proud. When you come home, I will tousle your hair and pour water in your eyes to wash the last of the tear gas away.

This is my work: to imagine the worst possible outcomes and the ways in which I will have failed in my actual, original work. This is how we move through the beginning of the end of days. This is how we bear witness to the slow unraveling. I will hold all of it with both hands. One for soothing, one to fight. I will take your abandoned cats, I will absorb your broken dreams.

The Land is a Calendar

There are friends who know where the bodies are buried. I have hands that know the earth: an intimacy that tells me that the ferns will come back to us. I know my son's tender fingers and I know their wisdom: where to dig for worms, plump and unhurried. They slither away from his tiny hands, but he is too swift.

The land is a calendar: Plums in July. Two months after that, there are apples and pears. Figs in October. In January and February, we pray for rain and let the grass grow as tall as it pleases. At the end of March, we put in the tomatoes. In May, the hummingbird builds her nest in the red flood of the bottlebrush tree, the one that lit up when I was away giving birth, rewarding me with its bounty upon my return. We turn water into life, rain into sacred fruit.

I have friends who eat the plum jam straight from the jar with a spoon. *It's the cardamom*, I tell them. It warms you from the inside. I whispered some black pepper into it as well, some spice for your soul. The sun on your kind face in the middle of winter. Holding your cheeks with the same hands that turn the dirt into something life-giving. The ones that bring things back to life. Eyes that turn to the sky to wait for the rain of fruit.

I was loved.

As a child, I was loved for getting up off the dirt (letting the adrenaline burn off, checking for breath, lifting myself to my feet, dusting walnut-colored dirt off my pants)—even by the classmates who were the ones who kicked me down in the first place, or shoulder-checked me into walls, or spat on me—and for getting back on the horse (even when the horse was not real, but instead a disappointing metaphor), and for taking it in the teeth while smiling and begging for more.

I was loved for my sharp wit and sarcasm and self-deprecation and the way I could turn the wolves of the conversation on myself around a high school cafeteria lunch table with such ferocity that people loved me out of pity in the vacuum of my love for myself.

After college, I was loved for putting my body on the line, for my ability to go too far, to shoulder risk and burden and blame and guilt and to overwork myself until my back ached and I took to my bed with a spine that gave in before my heart would, and marched with banners for a worthy cause in order to prove the same of myself until the soles of my feet were made concrete by the concrete. I was given a misdemeanor worth of love for a felony's worth of sacrifice.

And y'all won't fucking believe this, but before the dirt and the wolves and the risk, there was even a time when I was loved for my sweetness, the way I was seen and not heard—in dresses with white eyelet collars and patent leather shoes and itchy acrylic tights which have still not yet begun to break down in their landfill—and spoke only when spoken to and did not clean my plate but left a few bites to show my restraint and dutifully carried the dishes to the kitchen; I was loved for being hungry as I watched those last bites slip into the trash and for setting my hands in my lap in my grandfather's house to keep myself from touching anything and waiting for the grownups to finish talking before falling asleep in the car ride home against the window speckled with the reflections of brakelights.

And now, as implausible as it seems to me, I am loved whole and broken, covered in tear gas then tenderly stripped naked on the porch (to not track it into the house) and showered gently—and in the morning, I am loved with cups of coffee; in the evenings, I am loved with a hot water bottle at my feet and a cat in my lap and "don't get up" and the tenderness of a clavicle that fits the side of my face and invites me to exhale; I am loved without ownership: like an outlaw (not a citizen or a nation-state with borders or elections or currency or figureheads) belonging first to myself.

And only once I was loved that way, only then could I love myself like a precious bioluminescent cell in a vast ecosystem, holding the capacity for a teeming forest full of wonder and life and decomposition and trees that dared touch the sky in the palm of my hand.

Acknowledgments

Gratitude to the journals where excerpts of this book first appeared: *trampset, Milk Candy Review, The Citron Review, Nurture Literary, Paddler Press, Barren Magazine, Bending Genres, Corporeal Lit, Reservoir Road, The Hopper, Variant Lit, Dream Pop Press, Viridian Door, Vast Chasm, Autofocus, Ellipsis Zine, A Thin Slice of Anxiety,* and *JMWW.* I am eternally grateful to all the editors who have given my work such care to several of the pieces in this book. I could not have dreamed of this book without their encouragement. Special thanks to Jeff and *Stanchion,* who published the title piece of this book.

All the thanks to Ariana and ELJ for moving heaven and earth to make this book happen, and for your exceptional literary citizenship. To my pressmates, I'm humbled to be among you.

I owe so much to Melissa Faliveno and my Kenyon Writers Workshop crew. In addition to the parts of this book that came directly from our time there, the experience of being with you all will be an irreplaceable gift to my writing for the rest of my life. I am grateful to Hannah Grieco and Krys Malcolm Belc, in whose workshops with Catapult I wrote parts of this book.

My deep thanks to Esmé Weijun Wang for her kind words.

To my political community, my affinity groups, my chosen family: thank you for always giving me hope and leaving me more inspired than you found me. I love you.

This book is for my family. For Dorothy and Harriet. For Arlo, who is my constant source of delight and inspiration: thank you for teaching me to see the world in whole new ways. For my family of origin, who taught me to love words and the world. But mostly to Dan: thank you for the time and space to get this book written, and for believing in its inevitability. Loving me is no small feat. There is no book without you.

About the Author

Christy Tending is a writer, mama, and climate justice direct action organizer. A creative nonfiction editor at Sundog Literary, her work has appeared in *Longreads, The Rumpus, Newsweek,* and elsewhere. Her work received a notable in *Best American Science and Nature Writing 2023* and has been nominated for the Pushcart Prize and Best Small Fictions. She lives in Oakland, California with her family. She can be found at www.christytending.com.